IN SEARCH OF IDENTITY

IN SEARCH OF IDENTITY
THE JOURNEY WITHIN

DR. KENNETH URIAL GUTSCH

ReadersMagnet, LLC

In Search of Identity
Copyright © 2018 by Dr. Kenneth Urial Gutsch

Published in the United States of America
ISBN Paperback: 978-1-948864-20-6
ISBN eBook: 978-1-948864-21-3

All rights reserved. No part of this publication may be reproduced, stored in a retrieval system or transmitted in any way by any means, electronic, mechanical, photocopy, recording or otherwise without the prior permission of the author except as provided by USA copyright law.

The opinions expressed by the author are not necessarily those of ReadersMagnet, LLC.

ReadersMagnet, LLC
10620 Treena Street, Suite 230 | San Diego, California, 92131 USA
1.619. 354. 2643 | www.readersmagnet.com

Book design copyright © 2018 by ReadersMagnet, LLC. All rights reserved.
Cover design by Ericka Walker
Interior design by Shieldon Watson

ACKNOWLEDGEMENT

To my wife Nancy…my best friend…and my inspiration, I leave these last thoughts,

> We will meet again some day
> In a land far, far away
>
> A land we never knew before
> A land of love and much, much more
>
> We will walk among the oaks
> And share our love like all old folks
>
> I'll be waiting, don't be late
> This will be our final date
>
> We will never part again
> God will bless us both till then

Love, "Dad"

The Kingdom of God does not come visibly, nor will people say, 'Here it is,' or 'There it is,' because the Kingdom of God is within you.

—Luke 17:20—21

CONTENTS

Preface 11
Introduction.. 15

Chapter 1 As You Believe, So Shall It Be 17

              Who Am I, And Who Do I
              Want To Be?... 18
              Challenging Your Belief System 20
              The Stuggle Between Being
              And Doing 22

Chapter 2 In Search Of Truth 25

              Don't Kill The Messenger.......................... 29

Chapter 3 Expectations As Distracters 33

Chapter 4 The Values Of Right And Wrong 35

              Values: Struggling With Conflicts............ 37
              The Quid Pro Quo Of Relating 39

Chapter 5	Modeling And Shaping Beliefs	41
Chapter 6	The Path To Reality	45
	The Challenge Of Change	46
Chapter 7	The Choice Is Yours	49
Chapter 8	What Is Love?	59
	Is Love Eros? Philia? Or Agape?	59
	Is Love Axiomatic?	61
	Is Love Biological?	61
	Is Love A Fantasy?	62
Chapter 9	Sex And Love	65
Chapter 10	Life Experiences And Attitudes	69
Bibliography		75

PREFACE

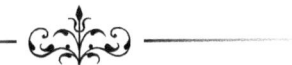

Life is a process. It begins with birth. Once begun, it continues on perpetually, perhaps as an extension of a universal force. There is no way to stop it, even though many have tried. The process is ours. It belongs to us, but we must first claim it as ours. That is, we must acknowledge that it exists. To do this, we must nurture our innermost thoughts, for what you are in your thoughts, you have become in your actions. To fight the process is to fight the power of the universal force. Once the die is cast, to fight it is simply to delay life's journey.

You might ask, "But how can I like the process when it brings me things I don't like?" The answer is simple: accept the things it brings you, and you will quickly move to a higher level of existence.

Change your perspective. The world presents all of us with multiple circumstances, but only as individuals do we decide what those circumstances mean.

Individually, nothing matters. The process of life is already in motion. What happens (IS) and now through time (IS NOT).

You have to understand that experiences lead to values, values to choices, and choices to a set of way thinking, a path to life.

The impact of those who touch our lives is of the essence. They become models for what we do and what we think. To change, we must reach our beyond where we are and discover who we are. We must listen to our inner thoughts and examine the accuracy of our interpretations of our experiences: am I reflecting someone else's opinion, or are these values truly mine? Are my choices really an extension of my belief system, or are they simply an extension of the values and beliefs of those who have shaped my life and served as models for me? How then do we change our path to life? We become enlightened when we realize that to change our lives, we must change our path to life. One way of doing this is through a reexamination of our experiences, our interpretations of those experiences, and the values we hold and choices we have made because of those interpretations. The process is intense and touches the area of psychology, religion, and philosophy, the impact of the Holy Spirit as the messenger of God and the ultimate truth of our interpretations as the gift of our efforts.

Nothing matters, unless, of course, we choose for it to matter. But why would we do that?

In philosophy, there is a saying, "In the absence of that which you *are not*, which you are *is not*." What that means is that without the experiences you have had, you cannot experience that which is yet to come. To hate the experience is a waste of time. But as I said before, the choice is yours. If you want to see what's waiting for you, you have to look beyond where you are. The interesting thing about relativity is that on a day in January when the temperature is 40 degrees, you might say it's warm; if, however, the month is May, you might say it's cold.

Life provides us with multiple experiences. The final decision on how to process them is ours. If you want to know what your gifts in life are, you have to open the boxes.

—Ken Gutsch

INTRODUCTION

THE WIND BLOWS WHEREVER it pleases; you may hear its sound, but you cannot tell from where it came nor where it is going (John 3:8). And so it is with life. The search for understanding begins with birth. There are no road maps to read, no paths to follow, no signs to direct us. There are only experiences to stimulate us, circumstances to challenge us, and impressions to taunt us. Both hope and fear are etched deeply into our minds as we reach to embrace a world we have never before known.

The journey we travel is long and arduous. The demands are great; the challenges, endless. We are touched by the love of those who nurture us, but disenchanted by their expectations. We are inspired by those who teach us, but disillusioned by their tunnel vision. We are motivated by those who lead us, but disappointed by their deceptions.

Our journey begins with a desire to know who we are, why we are here, where we have come from, and where we are going. Because the path of life has been paved by those who shape us, model for us, and teach us, we look to those same people for happiness, success, and comfort. But it is only as we journey within that we find our answers. It is only as we journey within that we realize that our thoughts hold the key to what we become.

We know that our belief systems are based on our experiences with others. Yet deep within, we know that what they have given us is not who we truly are.

This book details the inner journey we embark on as we move through life. It captures the essence of what we think and how our thoughts influence what we become. It addresses the impact of modeling and shaping on our lives and how such forces influence the values we have, the choices we make and the emotions we feel. It explores the circumstances we encounter in our search for truth and how that search impacts our belief systems. This is a book that provokes thinking about who we are and who we choose to be.

Chapter 1

AS YOU BELIEVE, SO SHALL IT BE

For as he thinketh in his heart, so is he.
—Proverbs 23:7

You cannot disembark from the journey of life. Your birth is the first indication that the journey has begun. The path you take will be shaped by those you love and those you hate, those who teach you and those who model for you, those who care for you and those who dislike you. The essence of your perspective (i.e., the way you see your life and your journey) will be touched by happiness and sadness, hope and despair, and satisfaction and disappointment. You will always be in motion. Once you have started the journey, there is no turning back; there is only understanding or misunderstanding, comfort or discomfort, and pleasure or pain. The path you take is yours; it becomes the core from which your perspective emerges, the very essence of what you think, what you say, and what you experience for the rest of your life. To change your life, you must change your belief system.

The task is arduous. You can think your way into a new way of acting or act your way into a new way of thinking. But the challenge to do so is, at best, unattractive. The rewards for remaining in the shadow of those who shape your life(i.e., your parents, your teachers, your mentors, your religious leaders, and those who are significant in your life) far exceeds the inner search for self-discovery. Following what others think, say, and do can easily place us in a situation where we can conveniently consider others responsible for everything and ourselves responsible for nothing. Thus, thinking your way into a new way of acting is not easy, but at worst, it appears to provide greater stability than acting your way into a new way of thinking.

WHO AM I, AND WHO DO I WANT TO BE?

Say for example, that you're on your way to work. How many times do you change your route? Not often, do you? Now suppose someone you respect tells you there's a much faster, shorter, and more aesthetic route. After thinking about it, would you take it? Probably! And if you took it and found it to be faster, shorter, and more pleasant, would you continue to take it? Thus, you would have thought your way into a new way of acting.

Suppose, on the other hand, that you had no desire to change your route to work but were simply formed that a five-mile stretch of road that you normally use to go to work is under construction and you'll be forced to take a new route. This creates some feelings of discomfort and anger. But it's something you are forced to do. Now suppose that route you take is shorter, faster, and more aesthetic than your original route and over time you find it to be more pleasant. Would you get over your discomfort and anger and continue to use this route even after the construction on your original route was completed? Probably!

In the first case, you changed your belief system because you thought it might be in your best interests, and it was easy to do because it was not in conflict with the values of those who are significant in your life. In the second case, you changed your behavior because you were forced to take a different route, and because the route was shorter, faster, and more pleasant, you changed your belief system and continued to take the route to work.

My point is simple. You have no reason to change your belief system without some provocation. Therefore, you continue to walk the path paved by those who influence your life. Is this good or bad? Not necessarily either: It only means that if someone said, "How would you describe yourself?" the adjectives you use would probably define for us the people who have touched your life and perhaps the extent to which they have touched it (i.e., the extent to which they have influenced your belief system). Thus, what you are and who you are is defined to a great extent by those who serve as your mentors.

The problem with being shaped is that when the desire for change arises and there is no one to follow (because what you are thinking is in conflict with what significant others in your life are thinking), then the struggle to find direction becomes frightening. The descriptive dichotomies with which have been indoctrinated tell us that something is good or bad, right or wrong, correct or incorrect, acceptable or unacceptable.

These dichotomies don't tell us how to make choices that are in our best interests and the best interests of others. All they help us to understand is how we have been shaped to feel about things. They are based on how others want us to be, how others want us to act, and how others want us to think. The most difficult challenge when facing change is that you are mentally walking through uncharted waters. The questions always remain the same: "Who am I?" and "Who do I choose to be?"

CHALLENGING YOUR BELIEF SYSTEM

The challenge to your belief system can come from many different directions. For example, there may be inconsistencies between what you've learned through your religious exposure and what you would now like to do as an adult, what you've learned in a class on ethics and what you would now like to practice as an executive officer in the company for which you work, what your parents taught you was right or wrong and what you saw as you watched them in action. These conflicts of interest pose some interesting things. Ultimately these thoughts turn into words, and eventually the words turn into actions. For example, one might ask, "How does one deal with the idea of premarital sex?" Society suggests abstinence, restriction, and control. But in reality, sex is a high-priority objective. Although the physical feelings are good, the societal previews are terrible.

"It's a sin!"

"It's for procreation only!"

"It's forbidden, and those who practice it will surely go to hell!"

How do we know what's right and what's wrong? The truth is that we don't. We only anticipate what others have told us. Thus we ask, "How do we make a choice?" and "What if the choice we make is incorrect (or ends in catastrophic circumstances)? Interesting questions, aren't they? We make choices within the confines of what we think we know. We seldom concern ourselves with the potential consequences.

Sometimes those who want us to make certain choices influence us in specific ways. Some suggest direction by siting religious passages, some with lectures on ethics, some with the use of drugs and alcohol, and some by rhetorical persuasion. And if what we decide to do doesn't work out, what then? We can always say, "The drugs did it, the alcohol did it, or all my friends do it!" Thus, the struggle to escape responsibility begins.

Obviously, escape mechanisms are a way of coping with bad choices. And bad choices lead to feelings of anger, despair, and hopelessness—with anger becoming the force, the power, the dynamic by which these feelings are communicated. And what is anger? Anger is an emotional expression that manifests itself in different ways. Most people experience anger at one time or another but deal with it in idiosyncratic ways. Some people become physically aggressive, others release their anger through verbal confrontation or withdrawal. It's not difficult to believe that we search for ways to justify our poor choices and that as we do so, we experience the anger that accompanies them. Then, too, with aggressiveness, promiscuity, and deception modeled for us every day on television, it is only reasonable to believe that expressions of anger will probably take a more violent form in the future. Anger, itself, is not so much the problem as the way it is expressed.

THE STUGGLE BETWEEN BEING AND DOING

But ultimately, the stuggle is between "being" and "doing."

What's the difference? Neal Donald Walsch (*Conversations with God*, Book 1, 1995, p. 170) has suggested that *doing* is a function of the body and *being* is a function of the soul. Whatever you're doing may be important, but what you're being while doing it is more important. Let me illustrate by paraphrasing a story I heard on the radio many years ago.

> While traveling through Europe, a friend of mine noticed a large excavation site. Curious about what was going on, he walked over to the site and called down to one of the workers.
> "What are you dong?"
> The worker responded, "Digging a hole!"
> Not satisfied with the answer, he went to the other side of the excavation site and again called down to one of the workers.
> "What are you doing?" he asked.
> "Building a cathedral!" the worker said.

Interesting, isn't it? Both men were construction workers. Yet one saw himself as the digger of a hole; the other saw himself as the builder of a cathedral.

Once you make a choice about where you want to go in life, the attitude you hold toward what you're doing is extremely important. The struggle between doing and being can create feelings of despair, inadequacy, depression, stress, and helplessness. These emotions are generated by our choices, the way we feel about them, and our ability to live with them.

It was Sigmund Freud (SE, 1915, vol. 14, p. 178) who suggested that people in conflict frequently use escape mechanisms such as projection, rationalization, displacement, sublimation, and regression to cope with poor choices. At best, the struggle to escape the immediate consequences of such poor choices is about all you can hope for. And when you have no direction, the consequences will probably be less desirable than you would like.

Interesting, isn't it, to find out how many different paths we can pursue in an effort to deal with our poor choices? For example we can: (a) project by blaming someone else, (b) rationalize by claiming insanity, (c) displace by kicking the dog, (d) regress by throwing tantrums, or (e) sublimate by diverting our emotions to more refined levels.

The problem is that inconsistencies in your belief system can lead to a set way of thinking that creates constant discord in your life. The situation can become iatrogenic (a situation in which the treatment is worse than the problem). Obviously, the question remains, "How does one make a choice which is compatible with one's personal life style?" Alfred Adler (Ford & Urban, 1964, p. 343) suggested that at least some of us use a technique he referred to as a safeguard. The idea is one of the avoidance. If you experience a situation in which you think you can't win or aren't competent, all you have to do is *avoid* that situation. The problem is that as you attempt to avoid things, you find that you're participating in very few things. This frequently leads to feelings of inadequacy, despair, stress, and depression. You have reached a point where what you are thinking is in conflict with what you are doing. The struggle to feel good about yourself is, at best, faltering. Some would say, "I can't give up my belief system, it's too important. It serves as an anchor for everything I think, say, or do." The response to such statement is basic. No one is asking you to give up your belief system. The idea is to modify your system until it becomes compatible with your highest objectives while not destroying the belief systems of others through lies, cheating, or deception.

Chapter 2

IN SEARCH OF TRUTH

"You will know the truth and the truth will set you free."

—John 8:32

Perhaps the essence of balance is truth. As you search for inner truth, you attempt to discover who you are and not who others want you to be, what your feelings are and not what others tell you they should be. But can we face the truth, and can we live with the truth we find? Philosophers have often suggested that the truth comes from within. Look within. Listen to your innermost thoughts. Learn to express those thoughts, and then act in ways which are compatible with those thoughts. Always maintain a semblance of harmony between yourself and the recipient of your thoughts. To do so creates an ambiance of peace. What you think becomes compatible with what you say, and what you say becomes compatible with what you do. The balance and harmony of your life touches all those you touch. All life's answers are within us. They become activated by our search, a journey of self-examination. They first become thoughts (i.e., special messages from within, messages that come to us through our senses, especially our intuitive sense). They then become words, and the words slowly transform to actions. Of all the senses (i.e., seeing, touching, tasting, hearing, smelling, and intuiting), the most important in this ambiance of understanding is the sense of intuition. The question then becomes, "How does one develop this sense?" A simple answer might be "Through meditation."

Unfortunately, that answer frequently leads people to believe that the goal of meditation is achievement. Thus, it implies that we can enter a tutorial class and rise through levels of achievement, each designed to take us to some higher spiritual goal. The real purpose of meditation, however, is to enter a state of awareness, a state in which we are receiving from our senses a perspective of life we have never before experienced, sounds we have never before heard, scents we have never before known, intuitions we have never before experienced.

And though this awareness, what is it you discover? The answer is simple. You discover who you really are and who you really want to be. You relate to a universality of existence in which all things come together. You begin to understand the significance of intentionality. You begin to realize the potential force of coming together—the strength, the power, and the resiliency of having all parts of a universal force moving together in harmony to accomplish an intended goal. The way to touch this universality is through harmony, truth, and acceptance—not through deception, aggressiveness, and hate. Interestingly enough, your past reflects on who you are and your path of life reflects on where you have been. One thing that becomes obvious as you travel this path is that the direction it takes you in today may not be where you choose to be tomorrow. They key to change in your belief system lies within the realm of how well it works. To find out, test it by playing the role of the pragmatist. Ask yourself how you feel when you're confronted with moral or ethical issues that you are based on deception. And when you conduct your own inner search for truth, what is it you find? Do you feel a sense of inner ecstasy? A sense of inner personal satisfaction that you have never before felt? An inner sense of self-esteem for having made a "correct" decision? (That is, a decision that makes you feel that what you have done is not only in your best interests but in the best interests of those with whom you relate.)

If not, you are, in all probability, experiencing a state of self-deception. What are you thinking is in conflict with what you are saying, and what you are saying is in conflict with what you are doing. William Shakespeare (*Hamle*t, act 3, scene 3, 75—77) put it better than most when he said:

> This above all; to thine ownself be true,
> And it must follow, as the night the day,
> Thou canst not then be false to any man.

What is it you win by pursuing truth? You harvest a journey through life embraced by an ambiance of inner ecstasy. You travel a path of life embraced by compassion and understanding. Because of your commitment to truth, the right thoughts, words, and actions will follow you wherever you go. You cease to kick against the circumstances in which you find yourself, for you know the truth has set you free. You become an observer of life, not a judge of circumstances, and when working with others, you encourage them with positive statements, not negative indictments. This then becomes a changed way of living. Some of what you have taken from the past remains, but that with which you touch the future is new. It is somewhat different. At first it creates a sense of separation, but in reality, it becomes a sense of unity, for nothing can come together and no unity can ever exist in the ambiance of deception. You cannot change the truth, but it can set you free. Deception is a path to self-destruction. Truth is a path to self-enhancement. Truth is knowing what to do. Deception is walking away from the responsibility of doing it.

Philosophers sometimes say, "There is nothing that does not exist." Meaning, of course, that even nothing is something. The fact that there is nothing that does not exist tells us by implication that to find the truth, you must search for it. That's probably somewhat like searching for snowflakes on Miami Beach. Nevertheless, once you've found it, the rewards it brings far outnumber the pains of deception.

Yet in the best interests of truth, it must be recognized that when searching for truth, it would be a mistake to believe that those who are deceptive are without some virtues just as it would be a mistake to believe that those who are honest are without some vices. The point is that the search for truth creates a sense of satisfaction within the person searching. The virtue of the search creates a sense of well-being. It is in sharing this sense of well-being that you gain satisfaction for yourself and harmony with others.

The question then becomes, "How do we pursue this search for truth while maintaining our relationships with those who have helped us to shape our past values and beliefs?"

DON'T KILL THE MESSENGER

Tread gently! To share your changing beliefs with others is probably a task more arduoud than your search has been. Those who love you, care for you, and support you are sometimes threatened, frightened, or angered by your desire to view ethics and morality in a nonpartisan way. To tell others who are significant in your life that you no longer support their codes of ethics or morals can become an extremely challenging experience.

If within the purview of discussing the discoveries you've made regarding your own self-examination you become insensitive to the beliefs of those who have loved you and supported you, then the changes in your belief system are, at best, terribly distorted.

The essence of change is to enhance the well-being of those who are in search of truth and those who become the recipients in discussing regarding the truth. Since discussions of this nature may be somewhat combative, it occasionally appears that the introduction of conflicting codes of ethics and morality lead to separation (i.e., provokes distance in the relationship). In reality, however, the foundations of any relationship based on truth should be more solid.

In practice, truth becomes the essence of unity, for unity can never exist in the shadow of deception. The challenge of course, is how the message of change is delivered. You've heard the phrase, "If you don't like the message, kill the messenger." In reality, what you say and how you say it always determines the outcome of your message. The way you deliver your message of change is as important as the change itself. Getting people to remain neutral (without intense emotional reactions) while examining a different set of morals or ethics is like trying to get a person who has just been snake bitten to remain calm. Fortunately, however, there is one big difference. With words, you can approach a subject as directly or indirectly as you wish.

Communicating with others is both an art and a science. The art of relating is in delivery, the science in the appropriate selection of words. People hate to have their belief systems attacked even if the attacks are justified. We like it when others encourage our thoughts, nurture our values, and support our decisions. So within this narrow frame of reference, it is necessary to remain sensitive to the values of the recipient. For example, when you're a teenager and have totaled the car, it isn't easy to go to your dad and say, "Dad, do you remember the car we used to have?" especially if your dad has a weak heart.

How then do you apply this wonderful art and science of relating? One of the things you might say is, "Dad, can we discuss something that's important to both of us?" Assuming he says yes (this creates some breathing space), you can then say, "I've got a problem. Part of it is mine, but part of it is yours. Last night, while driving home, I made an illegal turn on Twelfth and Madison, and as a result, a car in the eastbound lane hit us and damaged the left front fender. I've called our insurance company, and I've contacted the police department. I'll do what I can to pay for the damages not covered by insurance." Typically, a father will not be pleased to get this message. Fortunately, the message is couched within the framework of responsibility and honesty, and most fathers would appreciate that. The point is that messages must be delivered in a way that can be accepted by the recipient. When touching someone else's belief system or alluding to changes in yours, it is important to remember that you are *not in conflict* with someone else; you are simply sharing a change in the way you feel about your beliefs. Your intent is not to destroy the relationship but to continue it based on a different way of looking at morals and ethics. The bottom line is that the conversation must remain inclusive. It must reflect concern for both the person who seeks change and the recipient of such change. When this happens, your words become the instrument of change. Knowing how to communicate change while maintaining the relationship is a key in helping you to determine how successful you have been at changing your belief system while remaining in harmony with others.

Chapter 3

EXPECTATIONS AS DISTRACTERS

We live in anticipation of what is yet to come.

WHAT IF NOTHING IS right or wrong intrinsically but only seems so because you've been indoctrinated to think that way? What if we had lawyers without clients and doctors without patients? What if, as people, we had a world filled with peace, good health, and universal respect for each other? But can we expect anything like that?

Our lives are filled with expectations, and many expectations, at best, distort the search for truth, not because it's wrong to have expectations, but because what we expect is sometimes an imposition to those from whom we expect it. We expect people not to swear, but they do. We expect people not to have premarital sex, but they do. We expect people not to steal, but they do. And sometimes we expect people to be honest, but they're not. In effect, we live in a world of expectation, which at best is a challenge at and worst a disaster. So, expectation, as part of a belief system, leaves much to be desired.

On the other hand, the expectations we least like have a tendency to provoke our most intense thoughts, consume the greatest portion of our time, and shape our behavior most often. At first glance, it may not appear that way, but if you think about it carefully, you realize that the most tense moments of our lives are the moments that get the most attention. Ultimately, we spend so much time expecting failure that we have little time to concentrate on success.

Chapter 4

THE VALUES OF RIGHT AND WRONG

> Wide is the gate and broad is the road that leads
> to destruction…small is the gate and narrow is the
> roadthat leads to life.
>
> —Matthew 7:13—14

AGAIN YOU MUST ASK, "What if nothing is right or wrong intrinsically but only seems so because you've been indoctrinated to think so?" If this is true, how does one develop a value system? And are values and beliefs the same? Obviously, values and beliefs are not identical. Values are things we hold in priority, things that help others to understand who we are and what we believe. Beliefs are thoughts that become manifest through words. They exist as a defense system for our values. They are expressions of our values (i.e., our convictions) probably based more on the opinions of the people we value than on what we value.

Values exist as an extension of our support system. They imply, by our actions, that we have believe is right or wrong, good or bad, and acceptable or unacceptable.

Although not flexible, they can be and frequently are changed. The bottom line seems to be that it's difficult to change beliefs without changing values and that if you change values, you are probably in the process of changing your belief system. It seems that in practice, you can change your belief about a value, but only when you change your value will your belief system change. This, of course, is much like saying, "You can think your way into a new way of acting or act your way into a new way of thinking." However, with values and beliefs, the thought probably always precedes the value. Therefore, when making changes, it's important to look at how we see ourselves and others, how compatible these thoughts are with where we choose to go in life, and how we choose to be viewed by others.

Interesting, isn't it, how people come together in a climate which appears so volatile as our world does today? How can people live together, get along with each other, and create an ambiance of harmony within their group experiences? And what about marriage? How can marriage survive in a climate of conflicting values and beliefs? Not easy, is it? They key to survival has much to do with the truth. When people with conflicting views enter into a relationship, the truth may be the only basis for survival. Suppose that two people are considering marriage. One person considers sex healthy, invigorating, and pleasurable. The other considers sex gross, sinful, and repulsive. But they hold their values in check because they want to be married. Marriage offers a sense of security they don't have as individuals. Then, after the marriage, the truth begins to emerge until, finally, they find themselves in separate bedrooms. The challenge then becomes enormous, especially if your religion does not accept divorce. Some people would prefer not to step back from their religious beliefs. Thus, even though they dislike or hate the situation they find themselves in, they will not back off from the marriage. Their values, based on religion, damnation, and hell prevail over their desire for freedom, separation, and divorce.

VALUES: STRUGGLING WITH CONFLICTS

What happens within the confines of their belief system?

Obviously, they look for loopholes, ways in which they can be satisfied and fulfilled while remaining in a marriage that is disgusting, dissatisfying, and incompatible. A host of ideas seem to prevail. One justification for staying in the marriage is the desire to model marriage for the children (if there are any). Some model, huh? Another justification is a fear that one person will try to take all the money and leave the other person financially impotent! Still another is that it's better to live with way than go to hell! Or it's better to live this way than to live without security. Interesting solutions, aren't they? You find yourself in a situation originally based on deception. The original choice was between truth and deception. Now, several moths or years later, the choice is still between truth and deception. Can you live with your belief system? It doesn't seem possible, does it? How can you live with conflicting values and still satisfy your need for inner peace? The problem, at best, causes the persons involved to rethink their belief systems and/or to rethink their value systems.

One thought might be to change religions. That way, divorce might be acceptable and your new support system (i.e., the *new* congregation) will condone your new beliefs and your changed values. After all, when two people are incompatible, some would say divorce seems appropriate. Don't you wonder where the original feelings of love, caring, and compassion have gone? At best, you now have a new belief system and a changing value system. At worst, you have maintained your old beliefs and values and have changed religions for convenience—a way out. One might ask, "A way out of what, deception?" No, that's really not the way it works. The way it works is that your old belief system and your old values keep reminding you of who you really are (i.e., a deceptive person) and who you really want to be (i.e., a person seeking consistency within the confines of his or her thoughts, words, and actions). In other words, a person in harmony with reality.

Two forces that obviously impact your belief system are modeling and shaping. These two forces are always at work, and there are models to follow. After all, the law does stipulate that there is nothing illegal about consenting adults having any kind of sexual activity. So we look for models. One of the first avenues of escape in any situational conflict is to look at what others are doing. Where do you look? At great people, leaders, religious leaders, people who should *know* more about life than you do. The idea is, of course, that you can follow the model. That makes the model responsible for everything and you responsible for nothing.

If you want to know how well your belief system is working at this point in time, ask yourself, "What would the world be like if everyone did what I'm about to do?" For example, there are many who will argue that those who are leaders set the standards for morality and ethics. Therefore, because the world is changing, you have a right to exercise that change. However, what if your leader model acts that provoke immature and irresponsible thinking? After all, the law does suggest that personal privilege ends where public peril begins. That is, as individuals we can change but we must also consider how that change impacts others. Does that imply that if our leaders are deceptive, immoral, aggressive, and dishonest, it will impact the society in which we live? Not a pleasant thought, is it? A society based on deceptions, lies, dishonesty, immorality, and aggressiveness—just what the world ordered!

So how do you know when you are headed in the right direction regardless of where others go? Again, ask yourself, "If the directions I'm taking were followed by everyone else, what would the world be like?" If you don't like the answer, then perhaps the path you're about to take isn't the right path for you. The time to explore your feelings is now. Because the decisions you make are yours, the responsibility for those decisions are yours, and the consequences of those decisions are yours. What you have as your belief system will determine how you feel about yourself. It will ultimately define for others who you are and who you choose to be.

THE QUID PRO QUO OF RELATING

The outcome of your belief system and your personal satisfaction with who you are and where you're going will have much to do with your expectations. What is it you expect from the investments you're about to make? And how can you compensate for your losses? What we expect to win or lose has much to do with the changes we make. If we want a divorce, we must seek out individuals, groups, or organizations that believe in divorce. If we want premarital sex, we must seek out individuals, groups, or organizations that believe in premarital sex. And so on and on it goes.

If the people with whom we associate fail to bring us what we expect, we will look to other people for support. The question then becomes, "Will having a strong support system bring harmony to a belief system that is in conflict with itself?" The answer is no! Experience tells us that new thoughts and new ideas have to be tested against reality and then converted into reality with satisfaction to one's self and benefit to others. While this is happening, our support systems change. But how flawed is our reality? Are we in such a serious conflict within ourselves that we can't define it?

Chapter 5

MODELING AND SHAPING BELIEFS

> Lives of great men all remind us
> We can live our lives sublime
> And departing leave behind us
> Footprints on the sands of time.
>
> —from "A Psalm of Life" by
> Henry Wadsworth Longfellow

WHEN MAKING CHANGES IN your belief system, the choice is yours, the direction you take is yours, the commitment you make to change is yours, and the tenacity and resiliency with which you pursue change is yours. But because others have shaped you and modeled for you, the responsibility for success or failure rests with the impact that others have had on the thoughts you have, the words you use to express those thoughts, and the action you take to communicate those thoughts. It becomes obvious that the situations in which you find yourself are the situations that define for you who you are. And it also becomes obvious that through a process of self-monitoring, you will discover who you choose to be. In practice, it is simply a matter of monitoring cause-an-effect stimuli. Realistically, you set objectives and then determine what values must be altered in order to reach these objectives. This method of monitoring and altering continues throughout life. The purpose is, of course, to continue to do this until your thoughts, words, and actions are compatible.

New circumstances and new experiences in your life will always continue to challenge your present value system. And it is because we continue to grow and change that the way we view life (our perspective on life) changes. What seemed acceptable and true based on our knowledge of the past may not seem appropriate in terms of where we want to be in the future.

By moving systematically and basing the movements on truth, you will eventually find yourself in control of your life. The energy, strength, and power you gain from this systematic approach to life create an ambiance of self-esteem, self-confidence, and self-identity never before realized. The entirety of your energy can be focused on any project you undertake. The reason for this is apparent: there is no dissipation of energy through distractions (e.g., deception, dishonesty, and lies). You have nothing to hide. You have only to create, to envision that which you choose to be.

As it says in the Bible:

> Ask and it shall be yours
> Seek and ye shall find
> Knock and the door shall open.

The life you live is yours; it belongs to you. The direction you take in life is yours; it belongs to you. The truth with which you pursue your path through life is yours; it belongs to you. And the choice is yours, as are the consequences.

If you fail to pursue truth, your only alternative is deception, a condition for which you cannot claim ignorance.

Harmony in life is based on truth. It is not something you achieve; it is something you are. It is internal; it comes from a universal reservoir of truth, a reservoir of honesty, success, and hopefulness we tap into when we follow the path of truth.

To pursue this truth, you must envision your objectives and then monitor your thoughts as you move toward them. This is not a mental game. It is not a game of how hard you can concentrate on your goals, but rather, how well you can envision the steps you will take toward them. It is not an exercise in achievement; it is a commitment to realization. It is knowing that your are on the path to change and understanding how to get there.

There will always be distractions, but if the steps to your objectives are clear, you can reach beyond the distracters (i.e., people who will try to rob you of your self-esteem) and realize the goals you envision. In the advent of dissuasion, it becomes imperative to look beyond the negative thoughts of others and to focus on where you are going.

Monitoring your beliefs and values will keep you on track. Remember that beliefs and values are one. To exercise them to their fullest is to move toward your envisioned change. The ultimate truth in this case is that you are not a pawn controlled by outside forces but a free entity in search of self. By monitoring your thoughts and where you are going, you can move beyond these distracters. You can draw from a universal force, an inner force of power, strength, and confidence. You might ask, "How did this force get there?" The answer is, "You were born with it!" It is yours and always has been. You simply haven't exercised your right to it because there were so many people telling you to do what to do, how to do it, when to do it, and under what circumstances it should be done! And as you know, we are never bound by circumstances but only by choice. You are shaped by your thoughts, bound by your words, and judged by your actions. Those who see you look at you through the haze of their own infirmities. They see what they want to see, say what they want to say, and do what they want to do. But for the most part, they are programmed, and their thoughts are based primarily on the weaknesses of their own belief systems. They cling to the past because it is more convenient to follow someone else than it is to set your own course. They attack any thoughts, beliefs, or values that reach out to the future unless, of course, they decide the change will benefit their own deceptions.

This, however, is not your destiny, for you have, through your search within, discovered the path to truth and therefore, the path to eternal happiness.

Chapter 6

THE PATH TO REALITY

Give and it will be given to you.

—Luke 6:38

MAKING A CHOICE...THE PROCESS of selection is circumstantial. It is an extension of our values and beliefs. It is based on a process of decision making that takes us from where we are to situations other than the new ones we now experience. This does not imply situations that are better or worse, acceptable or unacceptable, and favorable or unfavorable. It simply takes us to situations other than the ones we are in. We probably expect that the choice will be good rather than bad, but the variables that lead to the future are always tainted by circumstances of the past. Therefore, making a choice has become somewhat of an art based on our ability to see ourselves realistically and a science based on our an accurate interpretation.

Making a choice is like placing a bet—the better you know yourself, the more statistically accurate you become in making choices that are in your best interests and the best interests of others.

The science of choice making lies in accurate self-examination and the honesty with which the results of that examination are applied to the choice. And what if the choice is bad? If your belief system is based on good thoughts, your choice will be good. If your belief system is chaotic and based on deception, your choice, in all probability, will be poor. The truth is that what is bad is bad, and what is good is good. The choice is yours, as is the evaluation. What is good or bad must always be so in terms of your own judgment. And how do we arrive at such judgments? Thoughts are harmonious when when we know them as truth, when they involve personal, positive gains for us and personal consideration for others, and when they are a reflection of a compatible inner world of thought and an outer world of circumstances. Yet, it must also be realized that while we are frequently eager to improve our circumstances, we are seldom willing to improve ourselves.

THE CHALLENGE OF CHANGE

Ultimately, to make a choice is to commit to change. But what circumstances lead to change? Do you change because of imposition or choice? Perhaps both! You change when you choose to be something other that what you are, when you have a desire to redefine your life, especially when things aren't going well. You also change because of imposition. Someone tells you to change and you do so or suffer the consequences. And so the change can be pleasant and comfortable or unpleasant and uncomfortable. But what about your belief system? How is that affected? Is the change painful? It can be! How do you change without pain? That may not always be possible! However, one way of changing without a great deal of pain is to project yourself into the change situation before it occurs.

Imagine yourself in the experience and how you choose to react within the experience. Visualize yourself in the experience. Ask yourself how you choose to respond to specific conditions within the experience. This exercise in preparation will desensitize you to the experience and alert you to many of the ramifications that can so frequently occur within a change of experience. Know what you are going to say and what you are going to do before the experience occurs. Understand what angers you and frustrates you, and envision how you can deal with those emotions before your experience occurs. Then practice with a friend who can stimulate those anticipated conditions. Do this and you will have taken a major step toward inner peace and personal accomplishment.

Remember that the path you are taking is one that you envision. It is a dream path. It exists in your thoughts, is defined through your words, and realized through your actions. To envision your goals this way is to take one step beyond them. The path to change has only to be defined. Your values tell you what direction to take, and your belief system tells you whether or not you have the awareness, resiliency, and self-confidence to begin this trip. It is a trip based on where you plan to go in life, how you plan to get there, and what you will do after you arrive.

Desires are aspirations are the stimulating factors. Desire is the path to choice, aspiration is the tenacity to stay on course, and thoughts are the essence of movement. As thoughts become allied to actions, the success or limitations of your change will be defined. Values will change when the change brings success, and the belief system will change when success is consistent.

Dreaming is the essence of hope. To dream is to permit your thoughts go to where they have never before been, to envision what they have never before envisioned, and to create what has never before existed. In the end, the dreams you have are yours and as you dream, so shall it be. What you envision is what you become. Your thoughts become your realities, and your realities, the sustaining force of your belief system. Ultimately, what you think is what you become. There is nothing more nor is there any less.

Chapter 7

THE CHOICE IS YOURS

No good tree bears bad fruit nor, does a bad tree
bear good fruit.

—Luke 6:43

WHAT YOU HAVE IN your world of dreams becomes yours because you believed it would become yours. It is yours because faith with which you embraced those dreams was yours and your journey within followed the path of truth.

And what causes our dreams to die? Is it fear that you can never touch the reality of those dreams, the fear that you don't have what it takes to complete the project? Maybe! Or is it that you don't know what steps to take to reach the dreams you have? Probably! It seems that life confronts us with unbelievable circumstances, some of which generate tremendous fear. Fear is usually a reflection of anticipated failure. Interestingly enough, the fear disappears rapidly when we face directly the objects we fear. Nothing is ever so scary as not knowing what to do, how to do it, when to do it, or why it should be done.

Fear is often generated by insufficient understanding. To face fear is to define what you choose to do, how you choose to do it, and why you choose to do it. The key step is to determine where you want to start and what your first step toward your dream objective will be. And what happens if you fail? Failure is possible! To avoid it, what you can do is build a back-up system. Id step number one doesn't work, try step number two, and if that doesn't work, try step number three. By pursuing a well-defined course of action the only way you can fail is to give up, to discontinue the dream simply because it consumes more time and effort than you're willing to invest. The choice, then, is yours. If the system doesn't work, change it.

The failure of a system does not constitute the failure of a person. It only defines for the person that which does not work. You can probably fill a book with stories of failure, but you can fill a library with stories of success. Interestingly, your belief system is the key to your success. The tenacity, resiliency, and assertiveness with which you approach the dream challenge will determine how far you travel. Unfortunately, when you arrive, you'll find the objectives you valued most are now only steps to new and more challenging objectives.

Naturally, you remain the architect of your fate. Your character simply emerges as you do the batter with your surrounding circumstances, and what can we expect as the battle ensues? Only you can define that. It remains a variable factor in your quest for self-esteem. The path you take in life (i.e., the choices you make and the way you make them) will make the greatest difference in where you go and how comfortable the trip is. It will not depend so much on what you are *doing* as it will on what you are *being* while doing it.

One of the truly interesting parables in the Bible (Matthew 25:14) is the story of a master and his three servants. It seems that the master had to go on a long journey. Because he was to be gone for along time, he entrusted some of his money (i.e., talents) to his servants for investments. To the first servant, he entrusted five talents, to the second servant, two talents, and to the third servant one talent. Upon returning home, the master questioned each of his servants regarding their investments. The first servant returned the five talents he had originally received, plus the five he had made through investments. The second servant returned the two talents he had received plus the two he had made through his investments. The third servant, however, had made no investments and simply buried the one talent he had received in the ground. Naturally, the master was well pleased with the first two servants but disappointed with the third servant.

Although the parable refers to money (more than two thousand dollars per talent), it's interesting to view the term *talent* in a different perspective. Assume for a moment that the world talent, instead of referring to money, actually refers to our special, but uncultivated, abilities. Then the message is somewhat of a documentary on how we invest in life. Because of his disappointment with the third servant, the master then said to his servants: "Take therefore the talent from him, and give it to the one who has ten talents. And the verse follows:

> For everyone who has will be given more,
> and he will have an abundance.
> Whoever does not have, even what,
> he has will be taken from him.

To take this statement literally would seem to imply that at east one purpose in life is to develop every conceivable talent we have. And this, of course, is a process of doing. What are we being while we are doing this would seem to give us some idea of how successful we are while we invest in life.

Being has much to do with character, and character has much to do with your belief system. Although the two are not identical, your character changes with your belief system. To say that you are the master of your fate is probably overstated. At best, you can search for your self-esteem or personal identity by pursuing the truth. But even truth seems to change as it becomes worn with time and frayed by circumstances. Ultimately, it is the search that matters, and it is the intuitive awareness of the person searching that matters. This, then, is the essence of truth. Truth is not a point in time but rather an attitude toward life and toward those with whom you relate. Truth is passion for moving in a direction which benefits you and those with whom you relate. And that direction is always an extension of your belief system. Once that system is on course, it is the intention with which belief system is driven that determines how comfortable you will feel while forming new relationships and exercising new beliefs. The greatest defeat system always to be among those who know not why they are here nor where they are going.

The world we are born into is filled with chaotic circumstances, horrific challenges, and personal doubts. It is a world in which personal strength, if it is to exist at all, must come from the inner unity we experience as we reach out for universal truth. Universal truth is like a mansion with many rooms. It consists of thoughts that have not yet been thought, words that have not yet been spoken, and actions that have not yet been taken. It is all that is, all that ever was, and all that ever will be. It is the beginning and the end, the alpha and the omega of life. It belongs to those who search for it and find it, those who recognize the purpose of life is not achievement but realization, that the search is internal and that those who seek shall find.

Unfortunately, many people are without support systems. If you have no love, no friends, and no relationships, it becomes natural to downgrade life. And if there is a person with whom you disagree, you denigrate him. If there is a philosophy with which you disagree, you trash it. If there are thoughts with which you disagree, you contradict them. And if there are ideas with which you disagree, you reject them. The bottom line is always the same: you think poorly of yourself; therefore, you think poorly of others. If others attempt to befriend you, care for you, or enter into a relationship with you, it becomes your contention that they want something from you. The challenge of a positive relationship is too great for you. If by chance, you enter into a close positive relationship, you must then worry about how to maintain that relationship. At best, the challenge of positive relating is too much for you. In essence, you have been denied self-esteem and have therefore attempted to deny others theirs. However, the uncertainty you feel within yourself at the moments like this is sometimes the path to a more secure and much healthier belief system.

The key to a better tomorrow is always to seek for something other than what you have. But the search must always be within. The choice must always be yours, and the results must always be in the nest interests of all those who are involved.

Albert Einstein once suggested that difficult problems could never be resolved at the same level of thinking at which they were originally introduced. To placate those who have shape your life is to follow the path you've just been on. To each beyond this path is to enter into a new realm of thinking.

You have no need to be encapsulated by the past when the future is begging to be touched. But there is always fear! The fear of failure, the fear of pain, the fear of loss, the fear of estrangement. And what is fear? Fear is a feeling of impending doom, impending changes, and apprehension. There is a decided difference between fear and caution. Caution is recognizing that diving into a swimming pool filled with two feet of water is unsafe. Caution is recognizing that playing Russian roulette and believing that fate will save you is ridiculous. Caution is realizing that you can't beat a train to a railroad crossing when you're both dead even in the race. Caution is realizing that you can't jump from a rooftop forty feet high onto a cement driveway without getting hurt. No, caution and fear are not the same. Fear is an emotion; caution is a process. Caution is a safety mechanism: fear is somewhat of a detriment. If we listen closely to our intuitive senses, we will know the truth, and the truth shall set us free.

Is fear ever good or bad? That depends! If someone is trying to convince you to dive into two feet of water from a ten-foot platform, fear is probably very good. If you're trying to learn to swim and your fear is of water, it's probably not very helpful.

Fear is a reaction to a given situation. At best, it is based on a belief system that is accurate and inclusive. At worst, it is based on a belief system that is chaotic and ego-driven. Most dangerously, it is nurtured by a desire to do things that are beyond reality, beyond the reach of your ability.

Fear, for the most part, is one of the most difficult emotions to understand. It exists everywhere, it touches everyone, and it is extremely difficult to define. Although it has never been defined in terms of faith, the idea seems interesting. In biblical terms,

> Faith is being sure of what we hope for and certain of what we do not see.
>
> —Hebrew 11:1

The idea leaves the impression that fear probably doesn't exist where faith is strong. But the idea poses some problems. Fear is not out enemy. It is an awareness that frequently teams up with caution and is brought to us through our sensory system. Is that good or bad? Actually, it creates within us a need for defensive thinking. In that respect, it's good. It's also good to know that through our sensory perception we receive messages that alert us to danger. It creates within us a need for caution. It is fear that alerts us to danger, and it is caution that helps us to move through the experience. Caution brings us to an awareness that says, "Tighten your security system." That's not bad. If we heed the messages from our awareness system, we eventually begin to rely on our awareness system as a part of our belief system. Is that bad? Probably not! Since most of the messages we get are far from less reliable sources (the outside world).

We need to recognize that fear is both biological and psychological. The difficulty is to distinguish or among the many approaches to resolve fear. On one hand, you have an emotional experience that, at best, is difficult to define. On the other hand, you have a biological problem, which, although you can define it, it poses other problems which you cannot embrace. For example, if someone asks you to dive into a swimming pool with two feet of water while standing on a platform ten feet above the water, the request might seem so idiotic that it generates no fear at all. The reason is obvious. The request is too stupid to take seriously. You cannot embrace an idea that is beyond the reality of your belief system. However, there are people who believe in confronting fear, regardless of the reality of the situation. Such people might take the challenge seriously. That very interest, the desire to face a fear object directly is what makes it necessary to understand the breadth of fear from rational to irrational and to differentiate between that which is feasible and that which is not. In other words, the idea of when and how to approach the object of fear is important in forming any belief system.

Fear is, perhaps, one of the most paralyzing emotions in us. To counter the impact it has on your belief system, you can monitor the conditions which it exists. Stimulate the conditions of fear at gradients acceptable to the person who experiences the fear and gradually introduce those gradients of fear in an effort to counter the condition feared. The approach is transcendent and can be applied to various types of fear but not to all types.

There are, of course, differences in biological fear and psychological fear. These differences create challenging circumstances that, in many cases, are idiosyncratic. Thus, to think that all fear must be confronted or that all fear can be counterconditioned is unrealistic. Your belief system embraces fear for obvious reasons; the most magnificent of which is to keep you alive and healthy, to make you cautious.

It is important to know that although fear can be incapacitating, the sense of caution it creates can be very healthy. But there are also times when it can serve as a serious distracter. There are moments in every person's life when he or she believes that something fearful is worth confronting, but there are also moments when confrontation could end in disaster. It is during moments like this that your belief system plays a major role in the direction you take, and how well you know yourself plays an important part in how successful you are in you approach to dealing with fear. If you are person of deception, the stigma of that deception will play an important role in how well you do. For example, you may believe that something is possible when, in fact, caution tells you it isn't or that something is impossible when, in fact, your awareness tells you to go for it. In both instances, the path you follow will reflect on the honesty with which you look at yourself and the honesty of your belief system. Therefore it is not difficult to believe that since fear is an emotion that occurs in the presence of anticipated danger, the extent to which you know yourself will determine how successfully you handle the conditions feared.

Chapter 8

WHAT IS LOVE?

Love is an emotion. To experience it is
exhilarating; to lose it devastating; never to have
known it is sad.

IS LOVE EROS? PHILIA? OR AGAPE?

AND WHAT ABOUT LOVE, the most dynamic of all emotions? How does it impact your belief system?

Love, like fear, is one of the most difficult emotions to define. If you don't believe it, pick up your dictionary and check it out. The definition of the word *love* probably consumes more space than any other single word in the entire dictionary. Yet when you finish screening all the definitions, there's not much closure. It's like asking,"Is the glass half full or half empty?" Philosophers have sometimes suggested different models of love. That is to say, different definitions for different occasions. For example, *Eros*, the Greek god of love, leaves us with the feeling that love and sex are one. That's probably the way love is most frequently expressed. Some philosophers might argue the point that eros can also refer to an aesthetic love expressed as people share art. Perhaps. But that's probably rare.

Philia, in contrast to eros is an expression of fondness for others. That probably means that we like others with whom we relate well. However, should the conditions of the relationship change, so will the relationship. It is a special kind of relationship in which the art of liking coexists with the art of being. You like someone because of the nice things they do or because of the nice things they say. Some philosophers have suggested that philia is an extension of the love you have for yourself. To some of us, that is an appealing thought. But when you analyze that thought, what does it really mean? Probably that if you can't love yourself, you're incapable of loving someone else. In other words, if it's not within the realm of your belief system, you simply can't express it, mostly because it is a love given freely and without conditions.

And what about agape? Agape is an unconditional, positive regard for God. That means there is no demand for reciprocity. Yet in Deuteronomy 6:5, the statement, "You shall love the Lord your God with all your hear, with all your soul, and with all your might," seems to be a statement of demanded compliance. Love is to be given out of obedience and only on a one-way street. However, in Leviticus 19:18, the statement, "Love thy neighboy as thyself," seems like the message we get in philia.

IS LOVE AXIOMATIC?

At best, this is pretty heavy stuff and seems to provide a challenging override on the ways we look at love. The biggest flaw seems to be related to how you understand love, how it is programmed into your belief system, and how your belief system has been shaped by circumstances.

The word *love* itself obviously implies different things to different people. So it is that just as your belief systems differ, so too does the concept of love differ. The truth off the matter is that the term is probably best defined as axiomatic; that is, it's self-evident. Each person has his or her own definition. It that's true, it might be important to find out what that definition is, especially if one person is using the term as a seductive tool and the other is using it as a path to marriage. Oh, you say, but we're not using the term. We're expressing our true emotions. Maybe! But then why are there son many unhappy relationships.

IS LOVE BIOLOGICAL?

On the biological side of the question, "What is love?" there are those who suggest that there are chemical overtones to love and the people who come together click chemically fist and then define what they feel as love later. Our guess would be that this implies a strong physical attraction for each other. Naturally, there are always those who would like to romanticize love, those who would like to think themselves into specific love relationships, because to do so gives them complete and total control over everything that happens in the relationship.

IS LOVE A FANTASY?

To dream or fantasize relationships is, of course, nothing new. People do it frequently because it's an exercise that permits them to move around within their belief system without anyone challenging what they're doing. The dream might be of a highly romantic relationship or possibly a wild sexual relationship. The interesting thing about fantasies is that you can do anything you choose, anywhere you choose, and any time you choose. As the dreamer, you not only have total control of what's happening but total control of where it happens, when it happens, and under what conditions it happens also. Nothing gets better than that! Or does it? The bottom line is that the thoughts are there, but the reality of the experience is missing. Not because it couldn't happen, but only because your belief system is monitoring what you can and cannot do. Even if you put your thoughts into words and your words into actions, you will miss the anticlimax of the fantasy.

Nancy Friday (1974) in *My Secret Garden* captures the struggle between fantasy and reality extremely well. It's interesting to see how some of the fantasies in her book are cushioned by certain specific realizations, reasons for submitting to the sexual acts within the fantasies (i.e., I was forced…I was on drugs…I was intimidated). What that seems to mean is that just in case the sexual fantasy isn't compatible with the propriety afforded by your mentors, your excuses have already been established. That's one of the appealing residuals of dreams or fantasies; they remain under control of the dreamer, and everything flows in perfect harmony. The problem is that the reality of the dream can't always be tested because it sometimes conflicts with the belief system to which you're shaped. So the struggle between what you might choose and what you finally commit to goes on and on and on.

So how is love defined? Is it a feeling? Maybe! Is it a reverence to God? Probably! It is a pleasurable experience? It can be! Is it a word frequently used as part of sexual intrigue? Sometimes! Is it axiomatic? Some people think so! Is it emotional? Definitely!

How would you define it? Probably as an emotional experience that relates exclusively to the belief system of the person who is experiencing it. It it reciprocal? Not necessarily! And because it isn't, the question of how belief systems come together becomes extremely important.

Albert Einstein suggested that the truth stands the test of experience. So it is with love. When belief systems come together, the experience becomes a test of integrity of those systems, and what causes the loss of attraction between two people who thought they were in love? One guess would be that in close relationships, deception lead to problem while truth leads to harmony.

> Whoever is dishonest with very little will also be dishonest with much.
>
> —Luke 11:9

Chapter 9

SEX AND LOVE

Man is a slave to whatever has mastered him.
—2 Peter 2:19

CAN YOU HAVE SEX without love? Of course! Do people actually do that? Of course! Why? Because they don't want people to know that what they're doing is in conflict with what they're saying. The facade they present differs from the thoughts they embrace. That is, they want their mentors to believe one thing while in reality they practice something else. Of course, they've probably already violated the tenets of their mentors by participating in premarital sex. But the bottom line is always the same; the inconsistency of thinking one way and acting another way leave you wondering who you are and who you choose to be. The deception is yours; it follows you throughout your life and creates within you as an ambiance of uncertainty, depression, and stress.

For those of you who consider life as a trial, it is that! And the reason is that the deception in the way you choose to live your life has created an internal struggle that's not easily resolved. You can't lie your way through life without some negative residuals.

Naturally, you struggle with the idea of how you can have, what you choose and still meet the basic tenets necessary for entry into heaven. After all, we all know that anyone who enjoys sex will surely go to hell. Right? Yet it seems only natural for people to exercise their attraction for each other and to desire close, loving relationships. Why would you consider this something you have to hide, unless, of course, it conflicts with the beliefs of your mentors. So how do you handle it? Change your belief system! When people come together sexually, the relationship is dynamic. If the relationship is agreeable to both people and does not violate their belief systems, then perhaps it's time to test the reality of the relationship.

Maybe the reality of the past is antiquated, worn out, along with the truth of the past. Maybe it's being challenged by the reality and the truth of the future. Maybe all religious leaders are not without sin; maybe all industrialists and chief executive officers are not without dishonesty; maybe our leaders are not leaders at all but people of pretense.

Perhaps the most appropriate question is, is your God a God of anger, wrath, and vengeance? Is this God you chose for your salvation? Seemingly, the choice is yours. What you think is what you get. If you believe in hell, it's yours; if you believe you're a sinner, you are! If you believe that your God is a God of love, understanding, compassion, and forgiveness, he is! Remember that it is a gentle God who talks with you through awareness. He is a kind and understanding God, who through awareness, helps you to make wise decisions. The key to understanding this is simple: you cannot be in a state of awareness (sensitive to God's presence) and be in a state of insensitivity to others. That's not the way it works! If you are insensitive to others, you can never develop an awareness of God. If your belief system embraces love, there can be no restrictions to the love it embraces. The more expansive the embrace, the greater is your awareness. The decision is yours.

So you see, love can be a rather dynamic experience. Is it something we should hide? Of course not! But there are consequences for deception. If the relationship is not in concert with your belief system, then the experience will be incongruent.

We are always in the process of becoming, and what we become has much to do with what we think and how we act. Are we acting out against God when we modify our beliefs? No! What you're really doing is acting out against yourself when you fail to modify your belief system. When your thoughts and actions come from your inner self (an awareness of the presence of the Holy Spirit), then the direction you are taking is on target.

> If you hold to my teaching…you will know the truth, and the truth will set you free.
>
> —John 8:31—32

Chapter 10

LIFE EXPERIENCES AND ATTITUDES

> For of all sad words of tongue or pen,
> the saddest are these:
> "It might have been."
>
> From "Maud Muller"
> by John Greenleaf Whittier

LIFE EXPERIENCES ARE CONTEXTUAL. They emerge from circumstances but always involve past beliefs. If you process these experiences in a way that is compatible with your interests, goals, and desires, they could serve you well. However, since some experiences are both circumstantial and contextual, you never really know which experiences will bring uncomfortable results, results with which you feel awkward, out of place, or shamed. The bottom line is always the same: the choice is yours, the results are yours, and the responsibility for that choice is yours.

Remember that the process involves disposition. It is a state of being. What you are being as you pursue direction in life is a powerful determinant of how much joy, comfort, and happiness you will find in life. Direction is important, but even more important is your attitude.

Your real challenges in life are within you. If it's true that the experiences you have are contextual, then it's equally true that how you feel about your experiences can create for you a climate of harmony or chaos. Attitude is extremely important. To be in a contextual state of becoming means that one of your challenges will be to embrace the best from each experience and go on with life. However, the way in which you process your experiences becomes extremely important. To accept them is to acknowledge them as important messages and guidelines to your future. To complain and agonize is to destroy them, and in fact, to kill the messenger (i.e., our sixth sense). Thus the attitudes we hold as we move through life have much to do with where we go and how satisfies we will be on the journey.

Remember that what you are being (your attitude toward what you are doing) determines your perspective on life (how you feel about life and how satisfied you are with who you are). The secret of happiness has much to do with your perspective. You can change your thoughts, beliefs, and your values much easier than you can change someone else's. thus, if you are unhappy in any given situation, it is always easier and probably more comfortable to look at the situation and change your perspective. If you're unhappy in a relationship, examine the relationship from a different perspective. If that doesn't work, change the relationship.

But don't run away from every relationship simply because it's not going your way.

Sometimes children dislike certain teachers or workers dislike certain bosses or managers dislike certain chief executive officers. The reason is usually because they do things differently from what their former teachers, bosses, or executive officers did. Unfortunately, you end up spending so much time thinking about "what was" that you cant' appreciate "what is." If, when you find yourself in a situation like this, you concern yourself more with what you have than what you had, the situation will improve. For example, a teacher or boss you had last year may have been very nice, and the teacher or boss you have now may be different. But you can't develop a healthy attitude toward what you have unless you spend less time looking at what you had.

Ultimately, it's like saying," I can't do that" (whatever "that" might be). The emphasis is on what you can't do. You "can't do something" because you've closed the door. Remember the door has not been closed on you, but *by* you. You've closed the door on yourself. It's like being on the starting block and hoping you're not the last one to the finish line. Perspective isn't everything, but in many cases, it's the only thing!

You can't improve the future unless you concentrate on the future. And if circumstances prevent what you expect or anticipate, then it becomes essential to change your perspective. Ultimately you can spend so much time agonizing over the past that you have little or no time to appreciate the present. That is indeed unfortunate. But the choice is yours. It's your mind. The thoughts are yours, and the process of dealing with them is yours. What you have is a reflection of what you think. If that turns out to be looking at the past and agonizing over it, that choice is yours. Whatever you give in life returns to you. Thoughts of failure bring failure. Thoughts of success bring success. You cannot build success on encapsulated thoughts of failure. And you cannot rise to success by thinking about what a failure you are.

How can thoughts of failure be pushed out of your mind? They can't! they must first go through transitions in your belief system. The transitions must be based on a different perspective, and the perspective cannot be based on pretense. You must believe in your mind, your heart, and your soul that these changed can be made and that they personify who you choose to be and where you choose to go in life.

The process is based on truth—knowing who you are and what you truly want in life. Exercise your thoughts about change by responding to a similar stimuli in different ways. How do you respond to others? If a friend is successful, do you become envious? If so, try this! Find ways to increase his or her success. How do you respond when a friend finds love, and you have none? Do whatever you can to promote the love your friend enjoys, and love will come to you. How do you respond when a fellow worker gets a promotion that you feel belonged to you? Do everything to help that person achieve success, and success will come to you.

Your attitude is a key factor to what happens in your life. If you choose to be a leader, then help others to rise to leadership positions. If you choose to be happy, embrace others with happiness. Ultimately what you give is what you get. And what you think is what you become.

Remember, the choice is always yours. Believe in yourself, and you will emerge from your cocoon of stagnation, and the future you embrace will be the most magnificent experience you have ever had!

BIBLIOGRAPHY

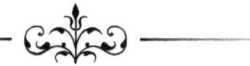

Ford, Roth, and Urban. *Systems of Psychotherapy*. (H B.Wiley & Sons, Inc., 1964).

Freud, S. *Instincts and their vicissitudes* (1915a) in *The Standard Edition of the Complete Psychological Works of Sigmund Freud*, Vol. 14, edited by J. Stratchey. (London: Hogarth Press, 1957).

Friday, N. *My Secret Garden: Women's Sexual Fantasies*. Pocket book edition, 1974.

Walsch, N. D. *Conversations with God: Book 1*. Hampton Road Press, 1995.

The New International Version of the New Testament. Zondervan Bible Publishers, 1973.

www.ingramcontent.com/pod-product-compliance
Lightning Source LLC
LaVergne TN
LVHW020434080526
838202LV00055B/5175